ShipWrecked
AND
RESCUED

CARS AND CREW

The "City of Bangor"

Copper Harbor, Michigan

Shipwrecked
AND
RESCUED

CARS AND CREW

The "City of Bangor"
Copper Harbor, Michigan

LARRY JORGENSEN

Fresh Ink Group
Guntersville

Shipwrecked and Rescued: Cars and Crew
The "City of Bangor"

Fresh Ink Group
An Imprint of:
The Fresh Ink Group, LLC
1021 Blount Avenue #931
Guntersville, AL 35976
Email: info@FreshInkGroup.com
FreshInkGroup.com

Edition 1.0   2022
Edition 2.0   2022

Cover design by Vicki Swisher
Cover art by Clyde Mikkola
Associate publisher Lauren A. Smith / FIG

Cataloging-in-Publication Recommendations:
TRA001050   TRANSPORTATION / Automotive / History
HIS036090   HISTORY / United States / State & Local / Midwest
(IA, IL, IN, KS, MI, MN, MO, ND, NE, OH, SD, WI)
ANT009000   ANTIQUES & COLLECTIBLES / Transportation

Library of Congress Control Number: 2022905527

ISBN-13: 978-1-947893-74-0 Papercover
ISBN-13: 978-1-947893-75-7 Hardcover
ISBN-13: 978-1-947893-76-4 Ebooks

Foreword

The stories of shipwrecks have fascinated readers throughout the world for generations. Many stories written include those that have occurred on the Great Lakes where there are over 6000 shipwrecks. Lake Superior alone accounts for over 500 with the loss of over 30,000 sailors. One of the most iconic is the wreck of the *Edmund Fitzgerald* in 1975 with the loss of its entire crew. Its legend will live on in the annals of maritime history.

I was asked by Larry Jorgensen to write the forward for his new book, *Shipwrecked and Rescued: Cars and Crew*. This newly published book revisits the story of the *City of Bangor* which occurred in November 1926. It was one of the most photographed shipwrecks around the Keweenaw Peninsula in Lake Superior. The *City of Bangor* contained a cargo of new 1927 model Chryslers and some Whippets destined for an auto dealership in Duluth, Minnesota. There was no loss of life but the crew suffered the freezing cold and snow causing frostbite as they were marooned on its shoreline for several days. By a miracle they were rescued by the U.S. Coast Guard who were in the process of rescuing the crew of another ship, the *Thomas Maytham* that went aground at Point Isabelle.

Due to the *Bangor's* position, aground in the shallow waters and lateness of the season, the salvage of the cargo of cars became a monumental task during the winter of 1926 – 1927. The cars eventually were shipped back to the Chrysler factory for refurbishing and redistributed to dealers for sale.

The hull would not be salvaged until the early 1940s along with another shipwreck the *Altadoc*. This ship went aground within a half mile of the *Bangor* in 1928. Metal was needed for the war effort during WWII and this led to a major effort by the salvage company.

A number of previous authors included a chapter written about the shipwreck, but most contained just the storyline. Larry Jorgensen has researched the various libraries and archival collections of maritime history. Having access to modern technology, he has been able to extend his research into the personal collections of descendants. This new wealth of information has allowed him to write an updated and more comprehensive book about the shipwreck with numerous photographs.

Being a trustee with the Keweenaw County Historical Society, I had the opportunity to meet Larry and assist him with his project. It has been said time and time again, "a picture is worth a thousand words". Larry has accomplished that with his new book *Shipwrecked and Rescued: Cars and Crew.*

2022
Mark F Rowe
Keweenaw County Historical Society
Trustee

Contents

Introduction

History has recorded many thousands of shipwrecks on the Great Lakes. However the wreck of the *City of Bangor* is like no other. It was not just the loss of another large steamer, it is an almost unbelievable story of the rescue of the ship's crew and cargo.

The *City of Bangor* was transporting 248 new automobiles from Detroit when a severe November storm on Lake Superior caused it to crash. It was tossed onto a reef off upper Michigan's northern-most point, the Keweenaw peninsula.

With that crash, the *Bangor's* sailing days on the Great Lakes came to an end as the ship was declared a total loss. But it was just the beginning for a three-month saga of an amazing rescue and recovery, and for a salvage operation eighteen years later, and finally for a part of the shipwreck story which remains on display at a lighthouse museum.

The 1926 shipwreck, while seldom mentioned in Great Lakes shipwreck stories or on shipwreck maps, remains an often recalled memory for many in the Keweenaw. People throughout the peninsula became an important part of the story as they responded to difficult challenges created by the disaster.

It has been said living in Michigan's upper peninsula creates survivors who are "the bravest, toughest and most friendly folks you'll ever meet."

It was those people who helped create one of the most amazing shipwreck stories ever told.

Chapter 1

STEAMBOATS AND CARS

Steam powered ships arrived on the Great Lakes one hundred years before the new and booming Detroit auto industry discovered the value that the ships could provide in delivering their new cars to anxiously awaiting customers.

The first two steamers, the *Frontenac* and the *Ontario*, were built in Canada in 1816. A group of New York businessmen financed the building of the *Ontario*, which they believed would be a successful venture on the Great Lakes, as another steam powered boat had been traveling the Hudson River and other waters since 1807. The Canadian built boats were designed to carry both freight and passengers.

The first U.S. built Great Lakes steamer was launched in 1818 in Buffalo, New York, and was called the *Walk-On-The Water*. The side paddlewheel ship was 132-feet long and provided 100 passenger cabins, a dining room, a baggage room and smoking room. The ship's unusual name was said to have come from the way it appeared when first viewed by native Americans.

All three of the first Great Lakes steamers were designs from Robert Fulton, who was credited with developing the world's first successful steamboat.

The ships grew in size throughout the 19th century responding to navigational improvements and new marine engineering developments.

Those first ships were paddlewheel driven, but by 1840 screw-driven propellers were introduced.

"Walk-On-The-Water" paddlewheel ship

Use of the steamers continued to grow so that by 1927 there were over 750 ships serving the ports of the Great Lakes, which is the world's largest fresh water area comprised of over 95,000 square miles. Lake Superior is the largest of the lakes with over 31,000 square miles and a maximum depth of 1,180 feet.

Shipwrecks on Lake Superior, according to historians, number over six-thousand. However, others say it's difficult to track the wrecks and the total could well be several thousand more. The National Weather Service has documented the month of November on Lake Superior as being the worst time for frequent severe storms, noting that waves can build higher there than on any other Great Lake.

The shipwreck of the *City Of Bangor* is not just another Lake Superior November tragedy. It is unlike any other in the long history of Great Lakes shipping. It is a near impossible rescue of men and cargo. It's an amazing story during winter's coldest months which involved communities throughout Michigan's northernmost peninsula.

Chapter 2

THE "CITY OF BANGOR"

The *City of Bangor* was built in 1896 at Wheeler & Company Shipyards located on the Saginaw River in West Bay City, Michigan. The shipyard was started by Captain Frank W. Wheeler and the *City of*

Bangor was the 113th ship to be constructed there. The shipyard was closed in 1908 after having built a total of 626 ships during thirty-two years of operation.

Bay County Historical Society

The "City of Bangor" launch – 1896

The *City of Bangor* was built for Eddy Bros. & Shaw, operating as Lake Transit Company. The ship was named after the previous home of one of the ship's owners, Jonathon Eddy who was secretary of Lake Transit. He also was general manager of Penobscot Mining Company, and a sister ship to the *City of Bangor* was named *Penobscot*. Eddy had moved from Maine to Bay City, Michigan in 1883.

The ship was 369-feet long when launched, but in 1905 it was towed from Milwaukee to a dry dock in south Chicago where it was lengthened. The vessel was cut in half and an additional 75-feet was grafted in at the middle to give the ship a new carrying capacity of two-thousand tons.

Lake Transport remained the owner and used the ship for transporting cargos of wheat, corn and iron ore.

The *Bangor* was one of three grain carriers down-bound from Canada in December of 1922, which became frozen fast in nine-inch thick ice in Lake Erie.

Several tugs worked for nearly a week to finally free the ships.

The Nicholson Transit Company of Detroit bought the *City of Bangor* and the sister ship The *Penobscot* in 1925, and the cargo loads for both ships soon would change. Nicholson had been organized in 1918 as an auto transportation company, and the 1925 purchase increased the company's fleet to ten ships.

In addition, Nicholson had recently acquired a tract of land on the Detroit River, which provided space for as many as 1200 cars to be loaded.

Automobile production in Detroit was skyrocketing in the 1920s, and much of the raw materials needed for the manufacturing was easily accessible and already being transported to the plants by Great Lakes ships. Iron ore, copper and wood came from Michigan and Minnesota. Steel was shipped from the great mills in places like Chicago, Gary and Cleveland and coal came from Pennsylvania.

The auto makers also realized Detroit's location between Lake Erie and Lake Huron provided convenient shipping for their new vehicles. To meet this growing need, steamers were redesigned to transport autos. A lower deck was constructed inside the cargo hold, and the main deck was made solid when the cargo hold openings were removed. Elevators were added to raise and lower cars to new lower decks.

By the mid 1920s Ford had established its own fleet of cargo carriers which would bring in raw materials and deliver finished autos. Other Great Lakes fleets were adding auto transport capability as more manufacturers recognized that the newly configured ships could deliver their autos to waiting dealers served by ports throughout the Great Lakes. Often when cars were sold to the dealers the price would only represent the cost of the vehicle on board, but the dealer would be responsible for the transport costs to his location.

Captain William Mackin came with the *City of Bangor* when the ship was acquired by Nicholson, and he was in the pilothouse when the ship set a record for delivering the largest single shipment of cars. It was August of 1925 when

*Pat Labadie Collection –
Alpena Public Library*

The "City of Bangor" at dock with cargo of cars in Chicago

Ken Thro Collection

**The "City of Bangor" en route to Chicago
with banner of record shipment**

The *Bangor* arrived at the municipal pier in Chicago with a cargo of 500 new automobiles. Captain Mackin must have been proud as the ship was greeted by a large delegation which included the mayor's office, the police department, auto clubs and area dealers who would receive the cars.

A large banner had been affixed to the ship's side proclaiming the new cargo record. Nicholson carriers also were easily identified by a large circular symbol painted high on the ship's bow. The logo was intended to represent an automobile tire.

The *City of Bangor* made news again on September 10, 1926, just a few weeks before the ship's final voyage.

It was in Grand Haven, Michigan where the press acclaimed it to be, at that time, the largest ship to visit the city's port. The *Bangor* had stopped at the N. Robbins dock where it was loaded with 42 new cars. This was part of a new plan by Nicholson Transit which would make Grand Haven a major port for the shipping of new autos. A newly paved road from Detroit was a major factor in creating the plan.

Three Nicholson ships were to be scheduled to serve the port, with the *City of Bangor* being the largest.

The *Sultana* had visited Grand Haven on September 8, and although it was shorter it could carry over 300 cars because of its three-deck design. The third ship scheduled for the plan was the *Senora*.

Thousands of cars were expected to be shipped from the Grand Haven port. The cars would arrive from auto plants in Detroit, Lansing, Pontiac and Flint to be transported across Lake Michigan to ports in Milwaukee and Chicago. Nicholson started another cross-lake Michigan venture in 1935 with a carferry service from Muskegan, Michigan to Milwaukee.

Chapter 3

THE "CITY OF BANGOR" FINAL TRIP AND ICY ENDING

It was November of 1926 when the *City of Bangor* was being prepared for what would be the ship's last cruise. It was being loaded with a cargo of 248 new Chryslers and a half dozen Whippet autos.

The Chryslers were among the first of the new 1927 models and were destined for the port of Duluth, Minnesota and for Chrysler dealers in the upper midwest.

The cars were the "entry-level" model #50, which the Pioneer Auto Company in Duluth was advertising for $750 for the coupe and $830 for the sedan.

The Chrysler name in the auto industry began in 1921 when Walter Chrysler was hired by the financially troubled Maxwell Chalmers Company to try to improve the company's operations. The company produced both Maxwell and Chrysler autos in 1924. The following year Chrysler and a business associate were able to acquire enough stock in Maxwell Chalmers to reorganize the company as the Chrysler Corporation.

Much of his engineering innovations carried with him to his new Chrysler Company, and the model years of 1926 and 1927 proved to be important growth years for the company. Chrysler became fourth in the auto industry in 1927 with sales of 192,083 vehicles.

The few Whippet autos loaded on board were manufactured by Willys-Overland in Toledo, Ohio. Whippets were built from 1926 to 1931 and ranged in price from $615 to $745. The Whippet was named after an English breed of dog, and the cars were recognized by a radiator emblem which depicted a leaping Whippet dog.

The ship had a crew of 29 men headed by Captain Mackin who was not concerned about being on Lake Superior with a load of cars during the stormy month of November. Mackin had sailed another auto carrier on the big lake just a few years earlier.

The *City of Bangor* left Detroit in late November of 1926 and traveled up Lake Huron, passing through the Soo Locks and onto Lake Superior on November 29.

However, the ship soon encountered severe weather with gale force winds and the near zero temperature which created ice six inches thick on the St. Mary's River, leaving more than thirty other ships frozen and unable to continue through the locks.

The quick weather change forced Captain Mackin to seek shelter in Whitefish Bay.

A day later the Captain believed the bad weather was abating and decided to pull anchor and continue on to Duluth. The ship sailed for only twelve hours and was nearing Keweenaw point when it encountered an even greater Lake Superior winter storm with blinding snow and stronger gale force winds extending for at least fifty miles. Mackin would later describe the storm as one of the worst he had ever seen as a ship captain.

The ship was unable to continue forward as the fierce storm caused it to roll side to side. The ship was riding high in the water because its cargo of cars had less weight than a regular freight cargo and The *Bangor* became more difficult to handle in the storm's heavy seas. The ship also was being powered by the same steam engine as when it was launched thirty years earlier.

Eighteen of the new cars which had been chained to the deck became loose and slid off into deep water. The lost vehicles had been secured with chocks placed in front and behind the wheels and then by a chain attached to each car and secured to a cable which ran the full length of the deck. When the cable broke the entire string of cars went over the side. A few years later that failed system of securing cars on deck was discontinued.

Captain Mackin, blinded by the snowstorm, mistakenly believed the ship had traveled past the Keweenaw Peninsula landmark of Brockway Mountain, which he concluded would place the ship west of Copper Harbor on the peninsula's north side.

The grounding site

Keweenaw Historical Society

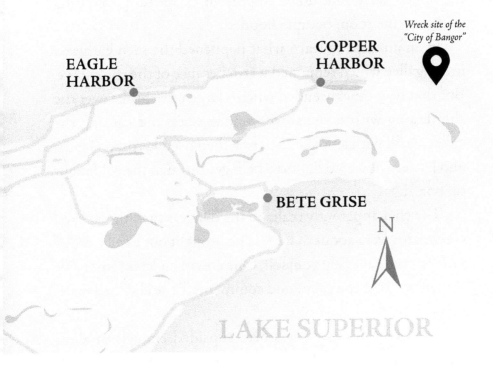

Wreck site of the
"City of Bangor"

COPPER
HARBOR

EAGLE
HARBOR

BETE GRISE

N

LAKE SUPERIOR

He decided to seek relief from the storm at Bete Grise, a bay located on the south side of Keweenaw Peninsula. In making the sharp change of direction he lost control of the steam steering gear, and in a final attempt to control the vessel he sent the first and second mates to the stern cabin where the auxiliary steering wheel was located. But they also were not able to control the rudder and all they could do was watch and pray as The *Bangor* headed toward the dreaded shoreline reefs about eight miles east of Copper Harbor.

A 12-foot gash was torn into the ship's side when it hit hard, about 200 feet off shore, at 6 pm on November 30th. The strong storm forced the Captain and his crew to remain on board that night and soon they were without heat because the boilers were shut down to prevent them from exploding as the engine room became flooded.

In an attempt to learn what happened the men gathered in the galley which remained warm because of the cook stove. But that heat quickly ended when a large wave broke over the ship taking with it the stove's smoke stack and causing the galley to fill with smoke. The crew then used kerosene lamps and battery powered lights to help get through the cold night on board.

The chef apparently realized the dangers his shipwrecked crewmates were about to face, as he brought out a full crate of oranges and said help yourself. One crewman later remember that incident in the galley and commented "the chef had never before been that generous".

The next morning the storm subsided enough to allow the men to chop away 8-inch thick ice to free a lifeboat, which was used to get them to shore.

The first group of eight men attached a rope to the lifeboat allowing it to be returned to the ship until all the crew and the captain were safely on shore.

Where they landed they observed a few cars which had become free from a secure cable and were washed ashore when the ship smashed into the reef.

One crewman later remembered seeing one car so badly damaged that he said it looked like "one ball of solid steel".

Once on shore the men were totally unprepared for the challenge to their actual survival they were about to face. The Keweenaw Peninsula is the northernmost point in Michigan, as it juts out into Lake Superior. The sparsely populated 50-mile long peninsula is blanketed every winter by heavy snowfalls, often accumulating annual totals of 300 or more inches. The men had no cold weather clothing or boots and some were wearing only oxford type shoes. As the weather worsened, they were unable to return to the ship for food or provisions.

Some started to develop frostbite, and with no shelter they decided to build a fire to try to keep warm that night. One of the crewmen thought to bring along a hand axe which was used not only to cut firewood but also for possible protection against the wolves. They heard wolves howling all around them and soon there would be volunteers to chop wood to be able to keep the axe close by.

The ship carried no wireless communications and no one knew they had wrecked, so the next morning the captain realized their best chance for survival would be to attempt walking to Copper Harbor. However the blinding storm had caused Captain Mackin to misjudge their location, thinking they were west of Copper Harbor. The men began trudging east through four-foot deep snow, while not knowing they already were east of the small community.

After several hours they realized the mistake and were forced to turn around and trace their steps back toward the abandoned ship. They would encounter wind blown snow drifts up to 10-feet deep making the travel even more difficult.

Some of the men had torn blankets into strips to wrap their legs and feet for protection against frostbite.

Their labored walking was made even more difficult by what ultimately became a failed attempt to take along the added luggage and personal belongings of four off duty captains who were included in the crew. The captains' ships

had been laid up for the winter in the lower lakes and they were hitching a ride back to their homes in Duluth. They brought their personal luggage ashore from the *Bangor* and several crewmen attempted to carry it along with their own duffel bags. But as the difficult snow trek continued the men became increasingly tired, cold and suffering from the growing pain of frozen feet. Slowly the captains' personal belonging were dropped or "vanished" into the woods, leaving a trail of items which later would be retrieved by scavengers. The men had spent 36 hours wandering through the bitter cold and snowy woods, and most were not sure how much longer they could survive.

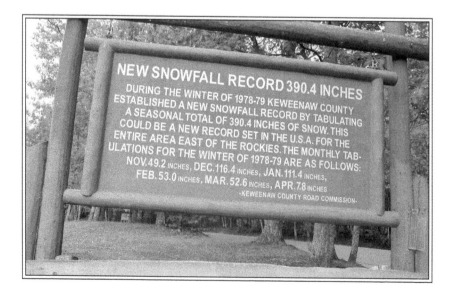

Keweenaw Historical Society

Chapter 4

"BANGOR" CREW FINALLY RESCUED

Another shipwreck caused during that same fierce Lake Superior storm set in motion a course of events which would result in the rescue of the desperate *Bangor* crewmen. It began when the 286-foot steamer the *Thomas Maythem* with a crew of twenty-two men became stranded on a reef while seeking shelter at Bete Grise on the peninsula's south side.

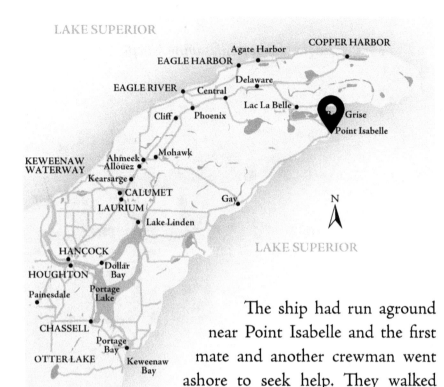

COPPER HARBOR

Agate Harbor

EAGLE HARBOR

Delaware

EAGLE RIVER   Central

Lac La Belle   Grise

Cliff   Phoenix   Point Isabelle

Mohawk

KEEWEENAW   Ahmeek
WATERWAY   Allouez

Kearsarge

CALUMET   Gay

LAURIUM

Lake Linden   N

HANCOCK   LAKE SUPERIOR

Dollar
HOUGHTON   Bay

Painesdale   Portage
Lake

CHASSELL

Portage
Bay

OTTER LAKE   Keweenaw
Bay

The ship had run aground near Point Isabelle and the first mate and another crewman went ashore to seek help. They walked for about six miles through shoreline snowdrifts until reaching the home of a commercial fisherman at Big Betsey River. The fisherman used his boat to take the *Maythem* crewmen to Gay, Michigan where they were able to locate a telephone. Their call for help went to the U.S. lifesaving station at Eagle Harbor where Captain Anthony Glaza then mustered his crew to begin the rescue.

While sailing toward the *Maythem* their rescue boat actually passed the site of the grounded *Bangor,* but heavy snowfall prevented the crew from seeing it and they continued their mission. All of the *Maythem's* men had been safely loaded into the lifeboat and were being taken to Copper Harbor when a break in the storm allowed them to finally notice the hull of the *Bangor.*

Captain Glaza circled the abandoned ship but after seeing no signs of any crewmen he continued toward his destination. However they traveled only a few miles when the *Bangor* crew was spotted struggling slowly through deep snow near Horseshoe Harbor. The captain steered his boat closer to where he could hail them to build a fire explaining he would then know their location when he returned after taking the *Maythem* crew to Copper Harbor.

Two of the lifeboat crew remained with the men from the *Maythem* to try to locate shelter for them with local residents. Copper Harbor in the 1920s was a small community of only a few dozen full time residents whose main activity was logging and fishing. The town was isolated during the long winter by continuous snowfalls which closed the narrow 39-mile road to Calumet.

One place at the harbor where some of the rescued could be accommodated was called "The Swedes", where four wooden structures had been built by two local Swedes, Fred Nelson and Pete Johnson who were seeking a business opportunity. The buildings included a boarding house, a saloon, and a blacksmith shop. The saloon building remains on the town's main street and has become a popular visitor's gift shop.

Before returning to the *Bangor* crew at Horseshoe Harbor Captain Glaza obtained a second smaller boat to assist in his rescue plans. He attached a line to the smaller boat making it possible to be pulled back and forth to the stranded men on shore. Several trips of the smaller boat were needed to safely bring everyone to the larger life saving boat. One of the rescued men later praised the captain for his smooth and skillful handling of the tiny boat in seas he estimated at fifteen or more feet.

The population of Copper Harbor increased by 52 people when the Banger crew arrived, and finding shelter for all the survivors became difficult. Some were housed at "The Swedes", but the search continued for additional much-needed shelter.

The Bergh family responded by providing space in their home for almost all of the *Bangor* crew and captain. Fortunately William Bergh had recently slaughtered two hogs in preparation for the long winter, and it also was said the Berghs had one of the best producing cows. One crewman remembered the experience as going to a small farm and said the breakfast of ham and eggs the next morning was "the best he had ever eaten".

Bergh Family Collection

The Bergh family home   *Ida Bergh*

*Snow covered
Bergh home
during winter
of 1926*

Keweenaw Historical Society - donated by Mildred Glaza

The men had been stranded for 36-hours without food, and Ida Bergh and her 14-year-old daughter worked in their small kitchen to prepare meals for their unexpected guests. They cooked for several days without hesitation, relying on the family's winter food supply, while not knowing if the food would be replenished before spring.

The task of guiding the frozen crewman to the Bergh home had been given to a son, 13-year-old Howard Bergh and his younger brother Albert. The two young boys were sent to "The Swedes" to lead the survivors on a half-mile walk back home. It became a difficult walk for the men, and years later Howard's daughter Martha would reveal her father's often told recollections of that experience.

She said "he couldn't understand why the men could hardly walk and would often fall down." Martha explained her father didn't realize they had spent the best part of two days struggling through hip deep snow, brush and swamps.

Those who earlier had wrapped their legs with strips of blankets discovered the snow had gotten underneath and formed ice around their legs.

The men were described as totally exhausted, dehydrated, frost bitten and hungry when they finally reached the Bergh home. They collapsed on the floor near the fire from a large wood burning stove, where they quickly fell asleep.

Howard's next task was to mop up the puddles of water which accumulated as the snow and ice began to melt.

Captain Glaza soon realized the small community would not be able to adequately support the needs of two rescued crews so he transported the men from the *Maythem* to the Eagle Harbor Coast Guard station. The weather conditions worsened and Glaza was unable to return to Copper Harbor for several days to determine what additional assistance should be provided for the men of the *Bangor*.

Glaza suggested also moving the *Bangor* crew to Eagle Harbor, but Captain Mackin ruled against the idea explaining that his men had suffered too much to again be forced to endure more travel on water. That idea also soon became unfeasible as the weather continued to worsen, freezing the the harbor solid and locking in the life boat at Copper Harbor.

Before returning, Captain Glaza had been able to place a call from Eagle Harbor to the hospital in Laurium and explained to Dr. Andrew Roche that he had shipwreck survivors in need of immediate medical assistance. The doctor was aware that a snow type vehicle was being developed by the local Chrysler dealer Paul Pawler who had modified a 1927 Overland model with a track type drive system and a set of skis for steering. The unique new creation proved to be a success as it pushed through thirty miles of deep and drifted

Keweenaw Historical Society

Pawler's snow vehicle

snow to transport the doctor to the life station. The vehicle next completed return trips to the hospital carrying some of the most seriously injured of the *Bangor* survivors.

Laurium Hospital

The Michigan House hotel

A horse and sleigh was next used to transport the remaining crewmen to the Laurium hospital until all available rooms were occupied. Others who were less injured were housed at the Michigan House hotel in Calumet where two area doctors would rotate shifts to provide needed medical attention. A memorial to the hotel's emergency service at that time is a current main floor display of two wooden wheels from a Whippet auto which had been part of the *Bangor's* cargo.

The head nurse at the hospital, Manila Gipp, later recalled her experience in caring for the survivors. She noticed that in their first days of care, they often would eat as much as a loaf of toasted bread with milk every day.

Wooden wheel display at the Michigan House hotel

As each man improved they were released and arrangements were made for return to their hometowns. Eight of the men were so badly frost bitten they remained hospitalized for two months. Four of them were from Detroit, two from Duluth, and one each from Saginaw and Cadillac. Theodore Dehlin was one of the men from Duluth, and later he may have returned to a great lakes steamer. The Dehlin name is recorded in 1944 as a steward on a ship owned by the Pittsburgh Steamship Company.

Another *Bangor* crewman, Harold Hartway vowed to not sign up for another ship. He had suffered severe frost bite and special treatment was necessary to save his feet. However he continued his forty-year career with Nicholson working on shore construction and other projects. He also married Captain Nicholson's niece.

Crewman George McNabb was uncertain about his future employment. However, he stated "the wreck made me sure I wanted to get off the ship".

The *City of Bangor* porter, Mike Wentz, vowed not to return to the lakes, but 30 years later he took a job in the galley on the *A.M. Byers*. Mike experienced a second shipping disaster in 1956 when he became the only crewman hurt when the *Byers* collided with the *E M Ford*. The *Byers* sank to the bottom of the St. Clair River.

It was believed that one or more of the crew remained in the upper peninsula after meeting future wives among the hospital nurses.

The *Bangor's* first mate Charles Hallett returned to his hometown in Bellevue, Ohio where he expressed his appreciation for the care he received in a Christmas card to the Bergh family. Ida's granddaughter Martha Lantz discovered the card in old family documents and has preserved it as a valuable record of Copper Country hospitality.

Bellevue Ohio
Dec. 20th 1926

Mr. & Mrs Bergh.

Dear Friends.

Just a X mas Card, to you. showing that I have not forgotten you. and also expressing some of my thoughts. of what you folks done for us. when we needed help badly. the night we arrived at your place. from the wreck of the Steamer City of Bangor. The crew is

*A note of gratitude
from Charles Hallett
to the Bergh family*

pretty much scattered now. and I am staying at my Sisters. and glad she was to see me I hear 5 of the crew are still at the hospital. but is being well taken care of. and I guess they will come out of it OK without serious damage. Well I hope Dear Friends that you will have a Merry X mas & Happy New Year the same as I expect to have. and that some time in the future. I will be able to meet you again.

although I hope in different circumstances than when I last saw you.

From Your
Affectionate Friend
Charles Hallett
111 Sheffield Street
Bellevue
Ohio

Formerly 1st Mate of Steamer City of Bangor

The little fellow who could not make much of a go on the skies, the morning we left.

Bergh Family Collection

Sheriff William Bergh

The Bergh family's service to Keweenaw didn't stop with the rescue of the crew from the *City of Bangor*. William was elected sheriff in 1937 and his family moved to Eagle River, the Keweenaw county seat.

Ida assumed a role of "under sheriff" and assisting at the county jail was one of her duties. It often was noted when a person was found guilty of an offense and given a choice of jail or paying a fine, jail time would be selected as Ida's delicious cooking was well known.

William was re-elected sheriff with his second term to begin January 1, 1939. Tragically he died just 15 minutes after the start of the new year. The sheriff had caught pneumonia the month before while providing help to a motorist during a severe snowstorm. Ida was named to complete her husband's term in office, and then went on to be elected to two more terms as sheriff of Keweenaw County.

With the health of the 29 crewman restored attention then became focused on the fate of over 220 new autos still locked in by ice on the abandoned *City of Bangor*. Just days after the wreck ship owner William "Cap" Nicholson and an insurance underwriter had secured the service of Paul Pawler and his "snow car" to take them to the site. After inspection the ship was declared a total loss!

Representative of insurance underwriter conducts inspection of wrecked ship

Glaza Family Collection

What was the fate of the *Thomas Maytham*, the other ship grounded on the peninsula by the same fierce storm?

After the storm subsided the tug *Favorite* was able to release the ship from its grounding and it resumed service on the Great Lakes.

However, just a few years later, the *Thomas Maytham* encountered a more serious situation when it struck a bridge on the Chicago river.

The bridge failed to open in time to permit the ship to safely go through resulting in a collision which removed the pilot house and everything else on the main deck. A huge pile of twisted debris had to be cleared away before extensive repairs could be made.

Main deck damage on the "Thomas Maytham"
after colliding with the Van Buren Street Bridge
on the Chicago River

Pat McPharlin Collection

Cars being removed from
The "City of Bangor" ship

Chapter 5

RESCUE THE CARS

What would become of the 220 new Chryslers which had become encased in ice on the deck and trapped deep below in the lower hold of the abandoned *City of Bangor*?

Walter Chrysler wanted his cars back and he contracted with the I.D.L. Durocher Company of Duluth to accomplish what became the most unusual and difficult salvage ever conducted on the Great Lakes. A representative of the salvage company, Duncan McPhail of Duluth arrived in Copper Harbor just a few days after the crew had been rescued.

He interviewed some of the men and then was able to initiate the first steps for the cargo salvage. The Durocher Company was to be paid $119 for each car removed from the wreck and returned by train to Detroit.

The cars were forced to remain on board for more than six weeks until water around the ship became frozen enough to support the planned rescue. During that time the salvage company constructed and manned a watchman's shack nearby to assure continuous security at the site.

Local workers also were hired to attempt to build an eight mile road from the remote wreck site to Copper Harbor. After carving a crude road of less than three miles through the dense forest, the road construction plan was abandoned when it was determined the cars could be driven on the shoreline ice with less difficulty.

Glaza Family Collection

Rescued cars driving on the shoreline

*The first crew arrives to begin work
on the snow and ice covered ship*

Keweenaw Historical Society

When the water finally froze solid a ramp of ice and snow was constructed to the ship's deck. The cars on top had to be removed first by workers using axes and other tools to chop away several feet of ice which had encased the exposed autos. The cars stored in the lower hold were in better condition and easier to remove. The head of the salvage crew, Duncan McPhail, believed it was urgent to work quickly as he feared the ship's hull could break under the weight of tons of ice which accumulated since the wreck.

Keweenaw Historical Society

The "Bangor's" deck elevator is covered with ice as the difficult task of removing the autos gets underway

The first cars were removed from the ship on January 25, 1927.

The cars began a slow and difficult trip to Copper Harbor which would be delayed at times by battery problems after it was discovered that some vehicles did not have working batteries. Consequently batteries had to be removed from cars which had completed the trip and then taken back to other cars at the wreck site. A few autos were so badly damaged when the ship crashed into the reef that they had to be hauled out on horse driven sleighs.

Glaza Family Collection

The trip to Copper Harbor begins

Houghton County Road Commission

Damaged car on sleigh

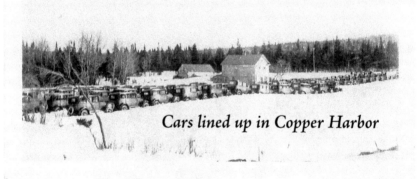

Cars lined up in Copper Harbor

Massman Collection

The final arrival of the vehicles in Copper Harbor created an amazing scene for the tiny community as all cars were lined up in long neat rows in Charlie Maki's barnyard. It was said that Captain Glaza of the lifesaving crew drove one of the first cars to the Harbor. Many of the photos of the event were likely taken by Glaza as photography was his hobby.

The total value of the cars at that time was set at $250,000 and Chrysler wanted them back in Detroit as soon as possible to be inspected, receive any needed repairs, and then sent back to the showrooms of waiting dealers. The plan was to have the autos loaded on railroad freight cars in Calumet, about thirty miles away. However, this was not to be easily accomplished as the narrow snow covered road to Calumet was not plowed open during the winter months.

The cars remained lined up in Copper Harbor for more than a month as road crews from both Calumet and Keweenaw counties were pressed into action to confront what became their most difficult winter challenge.

Thirty men worked around the clock for nearly three weeks to get the road open. The crew started plowing with a county-owned Wausau plow which became hindered by enormous snowdrifts and would create roadside snowbanks ten feet high. The men finally were forced to stop when they encountered snow drifts as high as twenty-five feet in the Lake Medora area, still several miles from their destination.

Houghton County Road Commission

At this point the road commission realized assistance would be needed, and they had learned of an experimental double rotary type plow which was being used in Albert Lea, Minnesota. Use of the new Edwards-made plow was obtained and it slowly pushed its way through the remaining difficult miles to Copper Harbor. Residents there were startled by the loud rotary drone sound made when the plow worked its way down the long hill into town.

It was four months after the wreck of the *Bangor* when the road to Calumet was opened. While the cars waited at Copper Harbor, gasoline was transported to them in specially constructed horse-drawn tanks on runners.

Glaza Family Collection

A group of eighteen cars were the first to arrive in Calumet at 10pm Sunday March 6, 1927. Wreckmaster Duncan McPhail drove the first car and reported the road as being in good condition.

The road had been opened that afternoon and the cars left Copper Harbor at 5pm. Those first drivers then returned to Copper Harbor and were able to bring another group of cars the next morning.

At that time additional young men were recruited to help bring the remaining autos to Calumet. The salvage company paid the drivers five dollars per car, and many of those drivers appeared to be school boys who had taken a day away from classes to earn the extra money.

The cars were loaded at the South Shore freight depot where an experienced crew from Detroit had arrived to handle the job. The loading was expected to go quickly with the completed shipment to leave early the next week. The total cost to remove the cars from the ship and deliver them to Calumet was reported as $35,000. The cost of the rail shipment to Detroit was estimated at $5,000.

The removal of cars from the *City of Bangor* was described by a local newspaper as "one of the outstanding events in navigation along the Keweenaw Peninsula".

It didn't take Hollywood long to learn of the "outstanding event" of the Keweenaw. A movie released just months later, in June of 1927, featured scenes of the winter road being opened to Copper Harbor.

Tom Keast Collection

Chapter 6

DID SOME CARS MISS THE TRAIN?

The new cars removed from the *City of Bangor* in January 1927 were scheduled to be returned to Detroit by rail as soon as possible.

But, did a few remain in Keweenaw after the train left the loading dock in Calumet? If so, how many and why are interesting questions which have fueled colorful stories told through the years about missing "mystery cars".

Judy Davis Collection

Whippet under shed

An often told legend hints that one or more cars eventually washed ashore to then be claimed by locals who discovered them. Another tale speculates that a car being driven to Calumet could have made a detour down a side road.

However, more tangible evidence exists to support the idea that some of the *Bangor* autos never left. One new car was so badly damaged by the ship's impact with the reef that the vehicle was reportedly sold for $25 to be used for parts by the local Chrysler dealer.

There also is the question about the fate of the few Whippets included in the cargo. If Chrysler was paying for the cost of the auto rescue and the train ride back to Detroit, would Chrysler pay to have the cars of a competitor saved? It's possible none of the Whippets ever left the peninsula.

Many years later a badly aged Whippet was revealed after being stored away in an old wooden shed at "The Swedes". When the shed started to collapse the car was sold for $500 by Wilbur Nelson, who it was said, had received the car from one of the Swedes.

Another Whippet was revealed in 1956 in a garage in Laurium. Copper Harbor historian and vintage car enthusiast Judy Davis purchased the Whippet at an estate sale which included the contents of the garage. It was believed when the previous owner was no longer able to drive, the Whippet had been stored in the garage prior to her death.

Proof of another Whippet can be seen at the Michigan House hotel in Calumet where two wooden Whippet wheels are on display. Again the question is where did they come from and what happened to the rest of the car?

Whippet car wheel

However what remains the most visible of the *Bangor* autos is a Chrysler which was owned for sixty-nine years by a family in Calumet. The car often was seen on the streets of Calumet, Laurium and other communities as it was being driven over 200,000 miles before it finally became a popular museum exhibit. The car was first purchased in 1927 from the Chrysler dealer by Andrew Slusarzyk who said he was told the car had been on the wrecked *Bangor*. When Andrew died four years later his brother John "Paddy" Slusarzyk bought the car from Andrew's widow. The car may have had a special meaning for the brothers as both worked for the highway commission which had cleared the road to allow the cars to be driven to Calumet.

Paddy loved the car and often drove it in parades and at other community events. He explained he would drive it every day during the summer months and in the winter he would frequently run the engine to keep it operating well.

Michigan Tech Archives

Paddy with car

John Slusarzyk (right) and Charles Belyan
of the highway safety commission's check committee.
Congratulates John for the car being the oldest
of 3,000 to pass the safety test. The 1927 Chrysler
had been driven over 200,000 miles at the time.

His dedicated maintenance of the car resulted in it recording over 200,000 miles of use, and it was recognized as the oldest of 3,000 cars to pass the highway commission safety test in the early 1970s.

John once boasted that even though the car was 45 years old, he wouldn't take a thousand dollars for it, despite its age. The car remained in the Slusarzyk family until John decided to give it to Andrew's son James who was John's nephew. However, James took little interest in the old vehicle and signed it over to his son Jim. Next the neglected car ended up in storage in Calumet as Jim moved to Wisconsin and was unable to take it with him.

The car's ownership finally left the Slusarzyk family in 1996 when local insurance man Art Vassold bought the old Chrysler for $5,000. Vassold had an interest in old vehicles and learned of the car being available from his business friend James Slusarzyk. The car was still in running condition and Art speculated he could restore it to increase the value. He later learned a full restoration would require extensive work and expenses and after five years he decided to again offer the car for sale.

News of the car being available caught the attention of Mark Rowe a trustee and maritime chairman at the Keweenaw County Historical Society. Mark had been a member of the society since 1983, but his fascination with Great Lakes shipwrecks goes back to his teen years when he would read old shipwreck newspaper articles which had been saved by his father. Later, while a student at Michigan Tech, he learned scuba diving and next he mastered the art of underwater photography, which became valuable skills as he increased his ability to learn more about the lake's submerged history.

The amazing stories of the *City of Bangor* became an early interest for Mark, and became even more intense after he met with the children of Captain Glaza in the 1980s.

Consequently, when the possibility of a car from the *Bangor* being available for display at the museum in Eagle

Museum display of photos

Harbor, obtaining that car became a priority for the society's maritime chairman. He already had spent years obtaining information and photos about the shipwreck and the difficult rescues of cars and crew.

However, Mark was not the only one to learn of the car's availability and to also express interest in its purchase. An official of the Keweenaw National Historical Park thought the car should be restored to be used for transporting special guests in parades and other peninsula activities.

Mark disagreed with the idea of restoration as he lobbied for the car to remain in its original condition and to be featured in an exhibit in the museum. He argued that restoration would remove important historical evidence including an axe mark which resulted from ice being chipped away to free the car from the *Bangor's* deck.

Mark Rowe Collection

Car on trailer to go to museum

Discussions between the two interested groups continued and resulted in the National Park representative finally backing away from the original idea of restoring the car. That decision opened the way for the Historical Society to raise the funds needed to purchase the car for $5,000 from Art Vassold.

In July of 2001 the *Bangor* Chrysler made one more trip as it was transported from Calumet to a new museum exhibit at the Eagle Harbor lighthouse. Rowe proudly called the car an important link to Peninsula history, noting that for years residents had talked about the 1926 shipwreck and the near impossible rescue of the crew and the cars. The museum exhibit includes photos and memorabilia which provide more details for those stories.

The captain's desk is included in the display as Captain Mackin apparently was able to claim his desk during the first salvage of the ship's operational equipment. The desk then was given to the Bergh family by a grateful captain in appreciation for the much needed care provided to his crew. The desk along with the captain's coat have been loaned for the museum display by the grandchildren of William and Ida Bergh.

The *City of Bangor* log book, an important record of the ship's last cruise, was believed to have been lost in the wreck

Keweenaw Historical Society

Captain's desk

CITY OF BANGOR SHIP'S LOG
J. M. Trotter started to find the wreck of the Bangor in the spring of 1927. Walking in the woods near the boat, he found a wide board beside a large log. The log book had been placed under the board by Captain Mackin during the storm the night the crew waded through the snow from the ship wreck. Trotter claimed that the last entry (now missing) stated, "We turned back to go into Bete Gris for protection ...then ... lost our rudder".
Given to Robert Skuggen in 1985 who donated it to KCHS

CITY OF
This dinner b
to Ada and F
by a crew me
which went a
Harbor on th
It was passe
Gregoire and
Nathaleen C
Keweenaw C

Log book

of 1926. But to have it suddenly appear nearly sixty years later was an unexpected surprise which started a chain of events to have the rare book being placed on permanent display at the museum.

A man named J. M. Trotter revealed that he had the book in his possession all those years after finding it near the site of the abandoned ship. He explained it was in the spring of 1927, just a few months after the ship had crashed onto the reef, when he and some friends decided to hike a few miles through the woods to locate the *Bangor*.

He said he was walking alone at the time when he noticed a wide board which had been placed near a large tree and under that board he spotted the log book. It was later thought Captain Mackin had placed the log there for safe keeping, planning to return at a later date to retrieve it.

Finally in 1985 Trotter decided he should do something with the old book, so he contacted the director of Keweenaw Tourism, Robert Skuggan in Houghton saying he would like to give the book to tourism. The tourism director then contacted the Keweenaw County Historical Society with news of the log book's discovery. The two groups made plans for the transfer of the book to the society in Eagle Harbor. A ceremony was held June 15, 1986 when the official log of the ship the *City of Bangor* was placed in the museum at the Eagle Harbor lighthouse. The captain's last entry in the log is "we turned back to go into Bete Grise for protection".

Coast Guard lifesaving crews who rescued the men of the *Bangor* and many others from Great Lakes shipwrecks are honored at another nearby museum in Eagle Harbor. The Lifesaving Museum is another historic site developed and

Lifesaving Museum

maintained by the Keweenaw County Historical Society. The museum is on the site of the original lifesaving station and is located inside the last remaining building, the station's former boat house.

Old boat inside museum

On display are several early wooden rescue boats including a completely restored 26-foot surfboat which was donated by a Wheaton College outreach program in Three Lakes, Wisconsin. Other museum exhibits feature the original equipment used in rescue missions as well as photos and memorabilia from the station's operational years of 1912 to 1950.

Once again the historical society's maritime chairman, Mark Rowe, led the effort to create the unique museum as he sought out and obtained the rare lifesaving artifacts featured in the exhibits. Together the two Eagle Harbor museums present a fascinating look at some historic Lake Superior events.

Mark examines the ax mark on the car in the museum

*William Bergh
visits wrecked
ship, sitting in the
gash to the hull.*

Bergh Family Collection

Chapter 7

A DIFFICULT
SALVAGE
OF MANY YEARS

The *City of Bangor* had been declared a total loss just a few
weeks after crashing into the off shore reef in November of
1926, and the crewmen were rescued after a two day struggle
for survival in the frozen and snow covered peninsula. All of
the cars were safely unloaded by the end of January. But what
would be the fate of the abandoned and badly damaged ship?
The final answer to that question would not be known until
eighteen years later after two salvage operations and a failed
plan to re-float the ship's hull.

The first salvage work at the *Bangor* began in the fall of 1927 with the hiring of the Detour Wrecking Company of Detroit. The salvage workers were able to remove the boiler and engines, important deck machinery and the pilot house, with all salvaged equipment placed in storage on Porter's Island at Copper Harbor.

During that initial salvage serious consideration was underway for a new mission for the *Bangor*. The large gash in the stern had been closed and improvised pumps were beginning to remove water from the ship's bottom. In addition, a guard was posted at the site to watch for any damage which might occur during the following winter months.

The new owners envisioned floating the hull in the spring by pushing the ship off its high position on the reef. The plan was to tow the hull down the lake to be converted into a barge for use in future wrecking and jettisoning operations on Lake Superior and Lake Michigan. However, their idea turned out to be unworkable because the storm had tossed the ship so high on the reef that the wrecking tug and barges could not get close enough. The efforts to re-float or accomplish any additional salvage work were abandoned in 1928.

Captain Mackin remained with the Nicholson lines until business slowed down during the depth of the great depression in the 1930s. Later the captain was employed by the Michigan state ferry system and finished his career as captain of the *City of Munising*, a passenger and car ferry operating across the straits of Mackinac before the big bridge was built.

There were no new salvage attempts for the *Bangor* after the Detour workers left the site, and the ship's hull remained

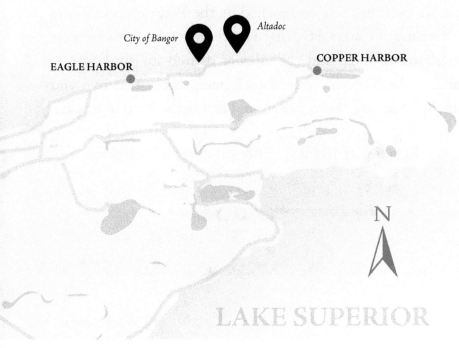

Sites where the two ships were wrecked

stranded on the reef for the next eighteen years. During that time it was a popular site for residents and visitors and became one of the most photographed of all Great Lakes shipwrecks.

Things would change at the shipwreck site in 1943 as U.S. participation in World War II created an urgent need for more steel to support war time manufacturing. That demand resulted in the K. H. Strait Company of Flint being contracted to salvage the hull of the *Bangor* along with the remains of another ship which was submerged nearby having been lost in a storm a year after the wreck of the *Bangor*.

The second ship, the 385-foot *Altadoc*, was an ore carrier built in 1901 and owned by the Peterson Steamship Company of Canada. During a fierce storm the ship's steering mechanism failed and the *Altadoc* drifted for six hours in huge Lake Superior waves until being broken in two and finally wrecking about a thousand feet from the *Bangor* site.

Remains of "Bangor" after cut down to waterline

Keweenaw Historical Society

Clarence Fisher Collection

Bull dozer pulling large bow section from Bangor

The *Altadoc's* engine room was flooded and all food supplies were ruined. Captain Simpson and four crewmen headed out on foot toward Copper Harbor to seek help, and because of the storm were forced to walk more than nine miles before finding a working telephone. Once again the lifesaving crew at the Coast Guard station in Eagle Harbor responded and were able to rescue the crew the next morning.

Before the salvage of the two ships could get started a road had to be built through the woods from Copper Harbor to the shipwreck site. Although the *Bangor's* hull was not deeply submerged a diver was required to help cut the ship into sections. Then salvage workers using acetylene torches worked above the water to cut the ship down to the waterline. The remaining submerged sections were pulled out with winches and specially designed vehicles.

The pieces of steel were stored on Porter's Island in a large temporary pile which some Copper Harbor residents described as "an eyesore". Similar salvage techniques were used next on the remains of the *Altadoc*. However, the pilot house of the *Altadoc* would serve a new purpose after it was hauled to Copper Harbor. The marine-looking structure attracted considerable attention when it became a small restaurant as part of the Pilot House Resort.

The Pilot House Resort

Truck with crane

After the Strait Company concluded their contracted salvage work, a second non-contracted "pirate-type" effort got underway to retrieve smaller amounts of steel which remained at the site. Two loggers who were working in the area set aside their axes when they discovered more money could be made by collecting and selling the remaining steel fragments than could be earned by their logging efforts.

Chester Lacasse and Randson Leblanc created a high rider type truck which included a crane and hook to assist their freelance salvage work. The unique truck was used to drag submerged pieces from the lake, and often an explosive charge was required to free the sunken steel.

The ambitious loggers may have been the last ones to find a financial benefit at the *Bangor* site, but the beach location remains a place of interest for marine historians and others who are curious about the shipwreck mysteries of Lake Superior.

Mark Rowe with timbers

Large timber which served an important use during the 1943 salvage work, has been exposed by high water. Marine historian Mark Rowe checked them out and explained the timbers had created a ramp which allowed dozers and trucks to be driven down to the beach.

Large pieces of *Bangor* steel were found in the sand by retired Captain Richard Metz of Eagle Harbor. Metz logged over thirty years of Great Lakes sailing experience, and in his retirement, enjoys underwater research and writing about interesting shipwrecks.

Large piece of steel in sand
Richard Metz Collection

Piece of steel under water

Mark Rowe Collection

One noted maritime historian who visited the *Bangor* wreck site is Ric Mixter an underwater photographer who has explored and recorded the stories of many Great Lakes shipwrecks. His TV documentaries have been seen by millions of viewers and he has been honored for his work. Ric's photography and knowledge of the *City of Bangor* have been a valuable resource in the making of this book.

Underwater photographer Ric Mixter

The *City of Bangor* may be gone, but it is far from being forgotten on Michigan's Keweenaw Peninsula.

"Senator" with cars on deck

Chapter 8

A "JINX" CARGO

Were new cars becoming a jinx cargo for Great Lake steamers? A reporter for the *Detroit Free Press* raised that possibility in an article he wrote in the spring of 1927 from Calumet. To support his theory the reporter noted that the *City of Bangor* wreck was the third incident in recent weeks which involved the transporting of new autos on the Great Lakes.

The other two ships he referred to were the *Westland* and the *Parks Foster*, each with a cargo of cars when they went aground. The *Westland* was carrying a cargo of new automobiles which had been loaded in Cleveland and Detroit. The ship became disabled by a broken propeller shaft while sailing on Lake Michigan about 36-miles northeast of Milwaukee, it's scheduled destination. The tug *William Meyer* was dispatched to tow the *Westland* to port.

The *Parks Foster* was being chartered by Nicholson Universal Steamship Company and was carrying 109 cars from Detroit to Green Bay when it became stranded by thick fog at Black River near Alpena. The ship was abandoned and declared a total loss. Later a salvage company had repairs made to the ship and the *Parks Foster* was put back in use until 1964.

The jinx theory probably surfaced again just two years after the wreck of the *Bangor* when another Nicholson Company ship met a tragic end while carrying 268 new Nash automobiles on Lake Michigan. The company had

Historical Collections of the Great Lakes
Bowling Green State University

The "Parks Foster" taking on a load of coal

Newly rebuilt "Senator" stops for fuel
at the Nicholson terminal

just recently purchased the S S *Senator* from the Spokane Steamship Company and considerable work was required to convert it to an auto carrier. It had been loaded at the Nash Motors plant in Kenosha and was steaming northward on the night of October 9, 1929 with new cars bound for dealerships in Michigan and other midwest locations.

It was foggy that night and the ship's crew heard the frequent fog signal from an ore carrier, the 420-foot *Marquette* which was headed south for Indiana Harbor from Escanaba with 7,000 tons of iron ore. Captain George Kinch continued to sail the *Senator* at full speed while also sending out fog signals.

The fog that night was described as "thick as pea soup" when the *Marquette* suddenly appeared just a few hundred feet away and headed for the *Senator*. Both ships attempted to turn away, but both turned the wrong way and the *Senator* was struck midship on the port side.

The *Senator's* SOS said the ship was sinking fast about 20 miles east of Port Washington. In less than ten minutes the *Senator* slipped beneath the waves and three of its 28 crewmen were saved when they jumped on to the *Marquette* immediately after impact. Others survived by floating on the wooden top of the ships aft cabin. The crew of a nearby fishing boat heard the collision and rushed to the scene where they pulled fifteen men from the icy water. Seven men, including Captain George Kinch, died in the collision.

What has become known as "the world's largest collection" of Nash autos now rests with the remains of the SS *Senator* some 450 feet under Lake Michigan.

The exact location of the ship and its cargo was determined June 10, 2005 and the site was added to the National Register of Historic Places. It also would be included in a National Marine Sanctuary, one of only two protected shipwreck areas in the Great Lakes.

Underwater shot of the "Senator"

The "Penobscot"

Pat Labadie Collection, Alpena Public Library

Chapter 9

THE "SISTER" SHIP

The *Penobscot* was a "sister" ship to the *City of Bangor*. Both ships were built at Wheeler & Company shipyard in West Bay, Michigan with the *Penobscot* being the 108th ship built there and launched in August 1895. The *Bangor* was the 113th built by Wheeler and was launched seven months later in March 1896.

Both ships were built for Eddy Bros. & Co., operating as Lake Transit Company. To understand the origin of the ship's names is to know more about one of the owners.

Jonathon Eddy, Secretary of the company, had moved to Michigan from Bangor, Maine and also was manager of the Penobscot Mining Company. Lake Transit used the two ships to transport cargos of wheat, corn and iron ore.

The ships were changed to accommodate shipments of new autos after both were purchased in 1925 by Nicholson Transit Company of Detroit. R. M. Leonard was captain of the *Penobscot* and stayed with the ship until it was laid up because of the depression in 1932. Crews were being laid off and the unemployment rate increased to over 25-percent. Those few ships still sailing often would operate with captains as crew.

The Nicholson auto cargo ships began to return to service in 1934, and within eight years all of the Nicholson ships had been converted to also transport bulk cargo.

The *Penobscot* was modified at the Nicholson yard where considerable work was done which included replacing the

The *"Penobscot"* in 1928

Massman Collection

The ship is headed up river with a load of grain

original wooden cabins with steel, changes to the deck and other improvements.

The company's need for non-auto cargos increased with the U.S. participation in WWII as the government ordered a halt to new car production. Only 500,000 cars remained stockpiled to be rationed only to people deemed in critical need, such as doctors, police and fire personnel, farmers and others in important public service.

The *Penobscot's* Great Lakes sailing days were impacted by a tragic collision and fire October 29, 1951 on the Buffalo River. A cargo of grain from Duluth had been unloaded and the ship with Captain Louis Guyette and

Captain Louis Guyette in the pilothouse of "Penobscot" before the disastrous fire in Buffalo, New York.

30 crewmen was being towed stern-first down river. At the same time the tugboat *Dauntless 12* was pulling the barge *Marania* which had left Toledo two days earlier with 800,000 gallons of gasoline.

Tug captain Thomas Sorenson did not see *Penobscot* until about 750 feet away as his vision was hampered by city lights

A hole punched into the barge

along the river. Putting the tug at full speed he attempted to cross ahead of the *Penobscot*. It was a failed attempt and although the larger ship had been able to slow down it was

Fire on the river

not enough and a hole was punched into the barge which ruptured two holding tanks allowing thousands of gallons of gasoline to spill into the river and fuel vapors to fill the air. Captain Guyette quickly ordered all portholes closed and cigarettes extinguished. However the scraping of metal between the ships created a spark which ignited the gasoline and the resulting explosion engulfed all three vessels in a 50-foot high wall of flames. Captain Guyette and wheelman Roy Richardson were killed instantly. Nine men from the tug and barge also died in the fire.

The blaze attracted thousands of spectators to the riverfront, as well as the Buffalo fireboat *Grattan*, the coast guard and other tugs and private boats to battle the fire.

The Hare Collection

From the Hare collection.

In Buffalo dry dock after the fire

Massman Collection

Grain storage

The fires on the deck and in the hold of the *Penobscot* were extinguished after several hours.

The *Penobscot* was towed to a Buffalo shipyard for repairs to the bow and stern and finally towed to the Nicholson yard in Detroit where damage to the ship was estimated at $200,000. After repairs, she sailed again on the Great Lakes for four years before being stripped of all equipment to be used as a grain storage barge in Buffalo. The ship was scrapped in 1963.

A Selection of Photos from

THE KEWEENAW COUNTY HISTORICAL SOCIETY

Ice-covered Chrysler cars on the "City of Bangor" deck

The "City of Bangor" grounded at Keweenaw Point

"Bangor" ice rail hatch

Snow-covered car

Cars are exposed – free of ice

Cars buried in snow

Cars begin leaving Copper Harbor

Cars travel the Lake Superior shore

A Chrysler car enroute to Copper Harbor

Museum log book exhibit

In addition to the Eagle Harbor Lighthouse complex,
the Keweenaw County Historical Society
operates ten other historic sites and museums.
Included are Central Mine, Eagle River Museum,
the Historic School at Gay, Phoenix Church
and Rathbone School.

Eagle Harbor lighthouse

The Eagle Harbor lighthouse and related museums at the light station have been maintained by the historical society since 1982, and the U.S. Congress transferred ownership to the society in 1999. Along with the lighthouse the site includes two former light keepers homes; the fog signal building, now a gift shop; and the maritime museum where the Bangor Chrysler and related memorabilia are displayed.

The lighthouse was built in 1871 and the light is still operated by the Coast Guard.

The winter site for the 1927 "gathering of Chryslers", Copper Harbor is also recognized for having the oldest lighthouse on the peninsula. In 1847, congress authorized $5,000 for the construction of a light at Copper Harbor. The need for the light had been created by increased Lake Superior shipping to serve the needs of the booming copper mining activity. The tower and a detached keepers house were built the following year.

A newer lighthouse with an attached dwelling was built in 1866. The station became unmanned when it was automated in 1919. The light was moved to a new 60-foot steel tower in 1937, and remains an active aid to navigation.

Summer visitors to Copper Harbor could rent the former keeper's dwelling from 1927 to 1957. The Michigan Department of Natural Resources acquired the property in 1957 and it became part of Fort Wilkins State Park.

Displays about the history of the light and area mining remain in the lighthouse, but the road has been closed and the best access to the site now is by boat tour.

Copper Harbor lighthouse
Archives of Michigan

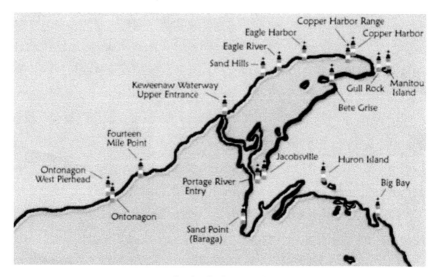

Peninsula lighthouse locations

There are eight lighthouses located on land on the Keweenaw Peninsula and another seven more off shore or on Isle Royale.

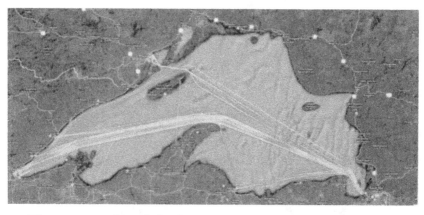

The importance of the Keweenaw lighthouses is revealed by this Lake Superior ship density map

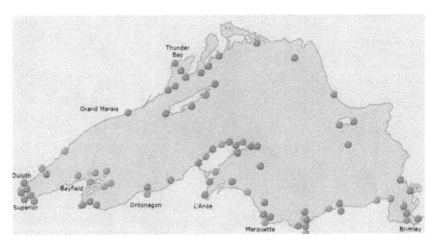

Lake Superior lighthouse locations

There are more than 75 lighthouses serving Lake Superior navigation, a number which has decreased in recent years as they age and the service is no longer needed.

Starting in 2000, the government has allowed the Coast Guard to sell off lighthouse sites no longer of value. Since then over 139 have been sold nationwide, with some being turned into private residences or museums.

Some sites simply have been abandoned, and an organization has been formed to restore and preserve them. The Great Lakes Lighthouse Keepers Association is based in Mackinaw City, Michigan.

It's often said "it takes a village". But it took a peninsula to create the amazing story of "The City of Bangor".

It was the determined people of the Keweenaw Peninsula who gave this unbelievable story a happy ending.

This book is dedicated not only to them, but also to those who have continued to keep the legend alive. It is appreciation to family members who have shared memories of tales told. To historians and archivists who have acquired and maintain the actual documents, photos and memorabilia.

And most of all to the remarkable "can do" tradition of Keweenaw people which makes this peninsula a safe harbor during troubled times.

About Larry Jorgensen

Larry Jorgensen first became fascinated with Michigan's Upper Peninsula and its unique history while writing and reporting for television news in Green Bay. However, his journey into that world of news had begun much earlier in northern Wisconsin where he worked during high school for the weekly newspaper in Eagle River. Later he was employed by a newspaper publisher in Milwaukee, and then on to radio and television news in Texas and Louisiana, along with wire service and freelance assignments. During all those years he looked forward to return visits to the Keweenaw Peninsula. During one of those visits, Larry discovered the tale of the wreck of the *City of Bangor*. Learning of that little-known event resulted in his decision to create this written account, which he hopes would share the story of one of Lake Superior's most unusual shipwrecks.

Fresh Ink Group

Independent Multi-media Publisher

Fresh Ink Group / Voice of Indie / GeezWriter / Push Pull Press

❧

Hardcovers
Softcovers
All Ebook Formats
Audiobooks
Podcasts
Worldwide Distribution

❧

Indie Author Services
Book Development, Editing, Proofing
Graphic/Cover Design
Video/Trailer Production
Website Creation
Social Media Marketing
Writing Contests
Writers' Blogs

❧

Authors
Editors
Artists
Experts
Professionals

❧

FreshInkGroup.com
info@FreshInkGroup.com
Twitter: @FreshInkGroup
Facebook.com/FreshInkGroup
LinkedIn: Fresh Ink Group

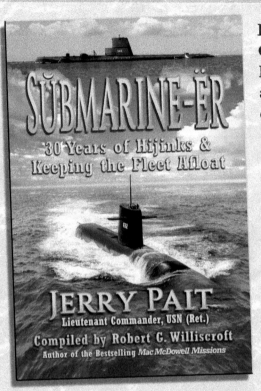

Lieutenant Commander Jerry Pait's semi-autobiographical collection of sixty stories recounts his thirty years in and around the U.S. Navy's sub- marine fleet. Ranging from light-hearted to wrenching, all are poignant inside looks at naval operations rarely seen by outsiders. Topics include the real story behind the shuttle Challenger tragedy, risking his own life underwater, discovering a Soviet spy living across the street, surviving when a DELTA Rocket engine ignites, critical missions, and the everyday lives of men and women of the fleet. Dive into Sŭbmarine-ër for hijinks and breathtaking adventure with this poignant memoir by a true American hero.

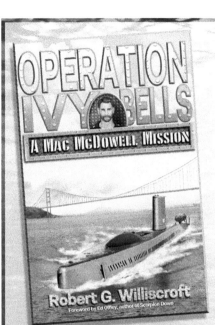
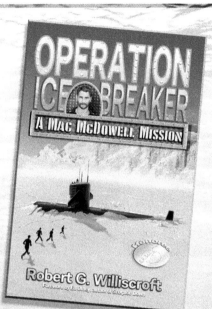
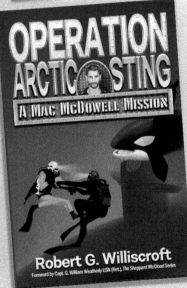
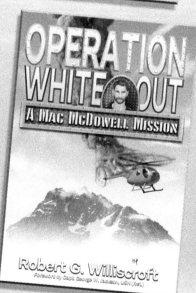

CPSIA information can be obtained
at www.ICGtesting.com
Printed in the USA
JSHW050732240123
36480JS00004B/8

9 781947 893740